99 WAYS TO FOSTERING INNOVATION AND CREATIVITY AMONG KIDS

DR DHEERAJ MEHROTRA

Contents

Preface   *v*

  1. 99 Ways To Fostering Innovation And Creativity   1

About The Author   53

Preface

The call for innovation and creativity has never been more resounding in a world of rapid change and continuous evolution. The complexities of our times demand fresh perspectives, novel solutions, and the ability to navigate uncharted territories with ingenuity. As educators, leaders, and learners, we stand at the nexus of this transformative era, tasked with nurturing the seeds of innovation and creativity in the next generation's minds.

"99 Ways to Fostering Innovation and Creativity" is more than a collection of strategies; it is a guide to cultivating a culture where innovation becomes a way of life and creativity is the compass that guides us through unexplored realms. This book delves into the multifaceted dimensions of fostering innovation and creativity in educational settings, offering a rich tapestry of ideas, practices, and insights that transcend traditional boundaries.

From reimagining classroom dynamics to embracing emerging technologies, empowering students, and fostering a growth mindset, these 99 ways encompass a spectrum of approaches catering to diverse learning environments. Each strategy is a stepping stone, a spark, or a catalyst to ignite the flame of creativity within educators and students alike.

The journey to fostering innovation is not a linear path but a dynamic exploration that requires adaptability, collaboration, and a willingness to embrace the unknown. As you navigate these pages, consider each strategy a potential beacon lighting the way to a future where innovation and creativity thrive as integral components of education.

This book is a testament to the belief that fostering innovation is not a luxury but a necessity. It is an ode to the educators who inspire, the leaders who empower, and the learners who dare to dream beyond the confines of convention. May these 99 ways serve as a compass, guiding you to unlock the boundless potential within every learner and educator.

Let us embark on this transformative journey together in the spirit of innovation and creativity. Here's to the limitless possibilities that unfold when we embrace the art of fostering innovation and creativity in education.

Author

www.authordheerajmehrotra.com

PREFACE

ONE

99 Ways to Fostering Innovation and Creativity

Encouraging pupils to think creatively and critically is one of the most important aspects of a great educational experience. We provide students the ability to think creatively and beyond the norm by encouraging them to develop these talents, which enables them to approach problems with novel solutions. Not only does it form a better comprehension of subjects, but it also goes beyond simple memorization.

The responsibility of fostering an atmosphere that encourages creative thinking and critical analysis falls squarely on the shoulders of educators. A few essential tactics are as follows:

One way to encourage curiosity is to provide questions that provoke thinking and encourage students to investigate things that interest them. This will help pupils develop a sense of wonder.

• 4 •

Regarding assignments, providing open-ended tasks for numerous interpretations and answers is essential. Students are allowed to build their viewpoints and solutions as a result.

Encourage pupils to work together to achieve the goal of collaborative learning. Working in groups provides students with the opportunity to be exposed to a variety of ideas and enables them to think critically about an assortment of perspectives.

Connecting classroom ideas to real-world settings is the fourth step in the real-world application process. Creativity is sparked in pupils when they can understand how the knowledge they are acquiring may be used in real-world situations.

One of the most important things to do is cultivate a culture that embraces errors and views them as opportunities for growth. The kids can overcome their fear of failing, and a *development mentality is fostered.*

Including reflective activities in the learning process is crucial to encourage reflection. To cultivate metacognition, you should ask pupils to reflect on their thinking.

Offer pupils various options to choose from when it comes to their homework and projects. Because of this autonomy, they can explore areas of interest, which helps them feed their

desire for learning.

Through these tactics, educators can develop an atmosphere that not only offers students the opportunity to acquire information but also provides them with the skills necessary to flourish in a constantly changing world. Education, creativity, critical thinking, and student development are all essential topics.

Without a doubt, the process of cultivating creative thinking and critical thinking is constant and ever-changing.

To further improve these talents in pupils, the following are some additional strategies:

Socratic Questioning: To foster critical thinking, Socratic questioning strategies are recommended. Inquisitive questions should encourage pupils to examine and evaluate the information given.

One of the tools that may be used for brainstorming and organizing ideas is mind mapping, which is introduced in this section. The use of this visual tool facilitates both creativity and the organization of thoughts.

• 9 •

Guest lecturers and Field excursions: To provide students with exposure to various views and real-world applications of their studies, bringing in outside lecturers or arranging field excursions is recommended.

Incorporating technological tools that encourage creativity, such as digital storytelling, multimedia presentations, or collaborative online platforms, is essential in integrating technology.

The use of project-based learning strategies, in which students engage in the completion of prolonged projects that are based on real-world scenarios, is essential. Problem-solving abilities and creative thinking are both fostered by this approach.

Debates and Discussions: Organize debates and class discussions on topics that are pertinent to the study of the subject matter. This not only improves one's ability to think critically but also the ability to communicate effectively.

One of the four components of cross-disciplinary learning is to encourage students to investigate the links between various courses. Because of this strategy that draws from several disciplines, they can better perceive the broader picture.

Establish a culture of providing constructive feedback. This is the first of five feedback cultures. Students benefit from this since it helps them polish their ideas, which fosters creativity and a critical attitude to their work.

Remember that the most important thing is establishing an atmosphere that highly emphasises curiosity, research, and careful analysis. Students evolve into lifelong learners who can negotiate the complexity of the world when they interact with these techniques throughout their students' educational careers. #Education #Creativity #CriticalThinking #StudentEngagement #Education Related Terms

Without a doubt!

The following are some methods that may be used to engage pupils in creative and critical thinking:

Engage kids in creative difficulties by presenting them with open-ended issues that demand them to come up with new answers. This may be accomplished via classes or tournaments that are held regularly.

Role-Playing: Incorporate role-playing activities into the curriculum to allow students to see situations from a variety of viewpoints, therefore simultaneously developing their capacity for empathy and critical thinking.

Reflective diaries: Instruct students to keep reflective diaries in which they may express their views, ideas, and questions on the subjects that they have studied. As a result, this encourages introspection as well as critical examination.

Encourage pupils to work together to achieve the goal of collaborative learning. Students may be challenged to think critically and creatively via engagement in group projects and conversations, which can result in a rich interchange of ideas.

Introducing real-world circumstances that demand problem-solving is the objective of the second problem-solving scenario. Students can apply their critical thinking abilities to real-world scenarios as a result of this.

As part of your literature review, you should include literature that questions the standard way of thinking. Students can build a more nuanced viewpoint via the analysis of a variety of literature.

Discussion of ethical problems and moral conundrums is the topic of the second item on the list. Students will be encouraged to think critically about values, consequences, and decision-making.

Inquiry-based learning is a method of teaching that involves students asking questions, doing research, and drawing conclusions on their own. It is recommended that classes be structured around this method.

Organizing seminars that concentrate on creativity is recommended to increase creative thinking. The activities that might fall under this category include design thinking workshops, brainstorming sessions, and creative activities.

Two to five years of experiential learning: emphasize learning via hands-on experience. Participating in activities based on the actual world helps expand one's education and stimulates innovative problem-solving.

Remember that the objective is to provide a dynamic learning environment that encourages inquiry, questions preconceptions and cultivates the skills necessary for effective achievement in a constantly changing world. Education, creativity, critical thinking, and student development are all essential topics.

Without a doubt! Students may be encouraged to think creatively and critically via the use of the following additional strategies:

We invite professionals from various areas to share their experiences and views, and we also invite guest speakers who are experts in their respective industries. The perceptions of pupils are broadened when they are exposed to real-world circumstances.

Socratic Seminars: To engage students in open-ended conversations, it is recommended to conduct Socratic seminars. Intellectual conversation and critical analysis are encouraged through the use of this strategy.

Mind Mapping: Mind mapping is a technique that may be used to develop thoughts and organize them. The use of this visual method not only fosters creative thinking but also assists in comprehending complicated ideas.

Encouraging cross-curricular relationships is crucial to foster linkages between various disciplines. Through this multidisciplinary approach, holistic thinking and innovative problem-solving become more prevalent.

During the thirty-first field trip, excursions to museums, scientific centres, or historical locations should be organized. The stimulation of creativity and curiosity from studying in various settings is a beneficial experience.

To cultivate a growth mentality, it is essential to emphasize the significance of having a growth mindset. You should instil in your kids the belief that intellect and talents can be increased through work, which will help them become more resilient and creative.

Student-led initiatives: Allow students to think and take charge of their initiatives. This autonomy fosters personal ownership, creative thinking, and critical thinking throughout the project.

Digital Storytelling: Incorporate many technologies that are used for digital storytelling. Not only does this raise students' levels of technical literacy, but it also allows them to express themselves artistically.

Using simulation games that involve strategic thinking and decision-making is a great way to improve your skills. These games provide pupils with a risk-free environment to experiment with various situations.

Discussions on Current Affairs: Involve students in conversations about important topics that are happening right now. Not only does this improve one's ability to think critically, but it also helps to relate what is learned in the classroom to the actual world.

Self-Evaluation: Instruct students to evaluate their work and encourage them. The act of reflection encourages metacognition, which in turn assists individuals in comprehending their thought processes.

It is important to remember that a lively learning environment that fosters creative and critical thinking may be created by providing your students with a mix of these tactics suited to their specific requirements. #Education #TeachingStrategies #StudentEngagement #EducationPrograms

Without a doubt! Students may be encouraged to think creatively and critically via the use of the following additional strategies:

To provide students with the opportunity to delve into issues in greater detail, it is recommended to assign open-ended projects. Independent inquiry, creative problem-solving, and learning are all fostered as a result of this.

This activity aims to organize debates and discussions on thought-provoking issues. Students are encouraged to explain their views, explore alternative points of view, and defend their beliefs as a result of this.

Inquiry-based learning, which involves students posing questions, conducting investigations, and drawing conclusions, should be the focal point of the courses that are structured around it. Curiosity and critical thinking are nurtured via the use of this strategy.

Collaborative Learning: Encourage cooperation through activities involving groups of people. The children are encouraged to share their ideas, learn from one another, and work together to solve challenges while working in teams.

Creative writing prompts should be included in the curriculum. These prompts should encourage students to think creatively and communicate their views in various ways.

In problem-based learning, students face real-world challenges that they must learn to solve together. This technique combines the ability to think critically with practical talents.

• 26 •

Introduce concept mapping as a visual tool for organizing and displaying information. Having this knowledge makes it easier to comprehend the connections between various topics.

Role-Playing: To immerse pupils in a variety of views, it is recommended to use role-playing situations. This contributes to developing empathy, creativity, and a more profound comprehension of various perspectives.

There is a method known as the Flipped Classroom Approach, which reverses the conventional classroom format by requiring students to study material at home and then engage in discussions and activities during class time. Active involvement and critical thinking are both encouraged as a result of this.

Encourage students to keep reflective notebooks in which they record their ideas, the insights they have gained, and the questions they have. A consistent practice of introspection improves metacognition.

It is possible to stimulate students' interest and critical thinking by demonstrating the practical applicability of the material they are studying.

One of the tasks that should be assigned to students is the curation project, which involves gathering and organising knowledge on a particular subject. Research skills are developed, and thorough analysis is encouraged as a result.

It is important to remember that modifying these tactics to cater to your pupils' particular requirements and interests is key to developing a dynamic and interesting learning environment. #Education #CriticalThinking #Creativity #TeachingMethods #Education #Conceptualization

Without a doubt! To encourage students' creative thinking and critical thinking, the following are some more strategies:

Invitations to Guest Speakers: Invite guest speakers from various areas to share their experiences and views with the audience. The pupils' thinking may expand when exposed to multiple views.

Activities that promote mindfulness should be included in the curriculum to assist students in developing their ability to concentrate, self-awareness, and emotional control. Having a peaceful mind makes it easier to think of inventive solutions.

Incorporate peer review sessions for student work, as the Peer Review recommends. The provision of constructive criticism from peers is a means of encouraging critical review and development.

Learning Stations: Establish learning stations with various activities associated with a particular subject. Exploration and problem-solving are both encouraged via the use of this hands-on method.

Introducing aspects of gamification into teaching is the objective of gamification. Engagement, decision-making, and strategic thinking are all something that may be improved via game-based learning.

• 32 •

Utilize TED-Ed lectures to investigate a wide range of subjects. These presentations often pique the audience's interest and encourage conversations on significant matters.

Passion Projects: Allow students to engage in individual projects to investigate subjects of particular interest to them. Having this kind of liberty encourages creative thinking and independent thought.

To enhance your visual thinking skills, it is recommended that you use tactics that entail examining and discussing visual art. Consequently, this improves one's ability to observe and fosters interpretation.

This activity aims to engage students in a discussion about current events and urge them to delve into these occurrences' ramifications and possible solutions. In this way, learning is connected to difficulties occurring in the real world.

• 34 •

Interactive Simulations: Incorporate interactive simulations or virtual laboratories into the curriculum to offer students hands-on experiences and stimulate exploration.

It is recommended to conduct Socratic seminars, including engaging students in open-ended conversations, to achieve the goal. Critical thinking, communication, and listening abilities are all improved due to this.

It is recommended to initiate activities that entail career exploration for career exploration. Students may be motivated to think critically about their future if they have a better understanding of the practical implications of their education.

It is important to remember to establish a classroom climate that is encouraging and welcoming to all students, one in which they may freely express their thoughts intellectually risky thoughts. These methods foster an environment that promotes curiosity, investigation, and profound thought. Education, Critical Thinking, Creativity, and Teaching Strategies are all essential topics.

Without a doubt! The following are some methods that may be used to engage pupils in creative and critical thinking:

It is recommended that debate clubs be established to provide students with the opportunity to participate in organized disputes. Their capacity to think critically, defend their points of view, and take into consideration competing ideas is improved as a result of this.

Collaborative Projects: Encourage students to work together on projects that require them to share ideas, solve problems, and work together to work together.

Introduce philosophical inquiry by asking open-ended questions. This is the step in the intellectual inquiry process. Students will be encouraged to investigate basic ideas and build their philosophical viewpoints due to these activities.

Role-Playing: Incorporate activities that include role-playing to allow students to experience multiple points of view and better understand complicated situations from various viewpoints.

Problem-Based Learning is a teaching method that involves designing classes based on real-world situations requiring reflective thinking and innovative solutions. Through the use of this technique, academic learning is connected to practical application.

The purpose of providing creative writing prompts is to encourage students to think creatively and communicate their views in novel ways. You may do this by providing students with creative writing prompts.

Interactive Quizzes: Instead of relying on passive memorizing, it is recommended to use interactive quizzes that require critical thinking abilities. Some platforms, such as Kahoot! Using Quizizz is one way to make learning more enjoyable.

Encourage children to keep learning diaries in which they may express their views, ask questions, and reflect on what they have learned. This is referred to as instruction.

Project-Based exams: Transition from conventional exams to project-based assessments, demanding students show their knowledge, creativity, and problem-solving ability.

Using mind mapping methods, you may graphically depict thoughts and concepts. This is the seventh step in the mind-mapping process. Students can better arrange their ideas and find connections between various components.

The Community Engagement Strategy focuses on connecting classroom learning to community challenges. Students should be encouraged to participate in community service or initiatives that solve local concerns to cultivate a sense of *responsibility and critical thinking.*

Peer teaching is a method that encourages students to assume the role of instructors by engaging them in the process of explaining topics to their classmates. This helps them build their communication abilities and strengthens their comprehension.

Exercises in Divergent Thinking: If you want to encourage pupils to develop diverse ideas and explore unusual solutions, you can use exercises in divergent thinking, such as brainstorming sessions.

Simulations and Case Studies: Include simulations and case studies that mirror real-world settings. Consider incorporating them into your curriculum. Students will be able to apply their academic knowledge to real-world scenarios.

Digital Storytelling: Investigate the many digital storytelling technologies that allow students to construct multimedia presentations, encouraging creativity in conveying their ideas.

Remember that you should modify these tactics according to the age group, the subject matter, and the specific dynamics of the classroom where you teach. One of the most critical steps in developing well-rounded persons is establishing a dynamic learning environment that places a premium on exploration, critical thinking, and curiosity. Education, Critical Thinking, Creativity, and Teaching Strategies are all essential topics.

Take pupils on educational field excursions to museums, scientific institutes, or locations of historical value. This activity on the list is towards enhancing critical thinking by engaging in learning experiences in various settings is possible.

Socratic Seminars: Conducting Socratic seminars is strongly recommended to engage students in conversation about complex texts or subjects. They will be encouraged to think critically, explain their opinions, and react to the ideas of others as a result of this.

Interactive Workshops: Organize interactive workshops and include guest speakers or experts with expertise from various professions. The students are presented with multiple viewpoints and the practical applications of knowledge.

Inquiry-based learning is a teaching method that involves designing lessons utilizing inquiry-based learning techniques. This method enables students to investigate subjects, ask questions, and engage in learning.

Using game-based activities to promote engagement and problem-solving abilities, including gamification in courses. This involves incorporating gamification into the curriculum.

Methods for Visual Thinking: It is important to use visual thinking methods to improve students' ability to observe and analyze. Some examples of these tactics include examining and discussing artworks.

Reverse Classroom Model: Implementing the flipped or reverse classroom model involves students engaging with educational material at home and using class time for collaborative and critical thinking activities.

Cross-Curricular Connections: It is highly recommended to demonstrate how ideas from several topics cross to foster interdisciplinary connections. Students benefit from this because it helps them grasp how information is interrelated.

Guest Lectures allow students to get exposure to real-world applications of their studies. This may be accomplished by inviting professionals or experts to provide guest lectures.

Presenting students with open-ended questions or challenges that compel them to think critically and come up with answers together is the goal of the problem-solving task.

Reflective Portfolios: Instruct students to keep reflective portfolios that chronicle their learning experience, problems encountered, and personal improvement.

The act of introducing coding tasks that not only teach programming abilities but also stimulate creative problem-solving is referred to as creative coding activity.

Cognitive Tools: Use cognitive tools and platforms that enable collaborative and creative learning. Some examples of such tools are Google Workspace, Microsoft Teams, and other educational technology tools.

The Flipped Inquiry method combines the flipped classroom approach and inquiry-based learning. This approach allows students to individually study subjects before participating in collaborative inquiry during class time.

The implementation of peer review methods for assignments and projects to develop critical assessment and constructive feedback among students is the subject of the evaluation.

Real-World Connections: Emphasize the connection of teachings to the real world, assisting students in comprehending the potential practical applications of the knowledge they are acquiring.

Students should be encouraged to participate in scientific inquiries, which include the formulation of hypotheses, the design of experiments, and the analysis of data.

Literature Circles: Organising literature circles where students read and debate works collaboratively is paramount to fostering critical analysis and interpretation.

Ethical difficulties: Present students with ethical challenges for debate, encouraging them to think about the moral consequences of their choices and make rational judgments.

Peer Collaborations: To enable students to learn from one another and gain from varied viewpoints, it allows students to collaborate on projects with their peers.

Feedback Loops: It is essential to establish feedback loops regularly, enabling students to evaluate their progress and set objectives for further advancement.

Global Perspectives: Incorporate global perspectives into teachings to cultivate a knowledge of other cultures, societal challenges, and international viewpoints.

Visual Analogies: When explaining complex topics to kids, it is helpful to use visual analogies to assist them in establishing metaphorical thinking and creative connections for the concepts.

Digital collaboration tools such as Padlet, Miro, or collaborative Google Docs are highly recommended for group projects and brainstorming sessions.

Student-Led Conferences: Incorporate student-led conferences into your curriculum, where students may display their learning, discuss their accomplishments, and establish their objectives for future learning.

It is important to remember that the objective is to establish an atmosphere that fosters curiosity, promotes inquiry, and instils a love of learning that will last a lifetime. Your students' needs and preferences should be considered while adapting these tactics, and you should have pleasure in promoting critical thinking and creativity in the classroom!

Teaching strategies, critical thinking, and creativity are in the realm of education.

About The Author

Dheeraj Mehrotra, MS, MPhil, PhD (Education Management)., a white and a yellow belt in SIX SIGMA, a Certified NLP Business Diploma holder, is an Educational Innovator, Author, with expertise in Six Sigma In Education, Academic Audits, Neuro-Linguistic Programming (NLP), Total Quality Management In Education, an Experiential Educator, a CBSE Resource towards School Assessment (SQAA), CCE, JIT, Five S, and KAIZEN. He has authored over 100 books on computer science, AI, digital body language, NLP, quality circles, school management, classroom effectiveness, and school safety and security. A former Principal at De Indian Public School, New Delhi, (INDIA), NPS International School, Guwahati, and Education Officer at GEMS, Gurgaon, with ample teaching experience of over Two Decades, he is a certified Trainer for Quality Circles/ TQM in Education and QCI Standards for School Accreditation/ School Audits and Management. He has also been honoured with the President of India's National Teacher Award in 2006 and the Best Science Teacher State Award (By the Ministry of Science and Technology, State of UP), Innovation in Education for his inception of Six Sigma In Education by Education Watch, New Delhi and Education World- Best Teacher Award, BOLT Learner Teacher Award by Air India, 'Innovation in Education Award 2016' by Higher Education Forum (HEF), Gujarat Chapter, among others. He has developed over 150 FREE EDUCATIONAL MOBILE Apps for the Google Play Store exclusively for Teachers, Students, and Parents. This work has been recognised by the LIMCA BOOK OF RECORDS and INDIA BOOK OF RECORDS as the only Indian to draw that feast. Dr Mehrotra is a PRINCIPAL at KUNWARS GLOBAL SCHOOL, Lucknow, India. He has conducted over 1000 workshops globally on "Excellence In Education" integrated with Total Quality Management and Six Sigma, Technology Integration in Education (TIE), Developing towards being ROCKSTAR TEACHERS, including Cyberspace, Cyber Security, Classroom Management, School Leadership & Management, and Innovative teaching within classrooms via Mind Maps, NLP and Experiential Learning in Academics. He is an active TEDx speaker and can be viewed on the YouTube TEDx channel. As a premium UDEMY Instructor, he has developed over 450 courses and caters to over 8 Lakh students from 180 countries. He can be visited at www.authordheerajmehrotra.com